D1737939

A TIME OF

BEES

MONA VAN DUYN

THE UNIVERSITY OF NORTH CAROLINA PRESS
CHAPEL HILL   1964

CONTEMPORARY POETRY SERIES

Copyright © 1944, 1953, 1954, 1956, 1958, 1959, 1960, 1962, 1963, 1964

by Mona Van Duyn

The first eight poems in this volume appeared with others in *Valentines to the Wide World,* which was published in a limited edition in 1959. "The Gentle Snorer," "Death by Aesthetics," "Three Valentines to the Wide World," "A Kind of Music," "A Serious Case," "Recovery," "Elementary Attitudes," "The Gardener to His God," "Open Letter, Personal," "A Time of Bees," and "A Garland for Christopher Smart" originally appeared in *Poetry.* Other poems in this volume have been published in *The Sewanee Review, The Kenyon Review, Perspective, Poetry Northwest, The Transatlantic Review, The Carleton Miscellany, Midland,* and *A New Anthology of American Verse.*

Library of Congress Catalog Card Number 64-16839

PRINTED BY THE SEEMAN PRINTERY, DURHAM, NORTH CAROLINA

Manufactured in the United States of America

To my family and friends,
in this world and the others

CONTENTS

I. VALENTINES TO THE WIDE WORLD

THREE VALENTINES TO THE WIDE WORLD

I

THE CHILD disturbs our view. Tow-head bent, she
stands on one leg and folds up the other. She is listening
to the sound of her fingernail on a scab on her knee.
If I were her mother I would think right now of the chastening
that ridiculous arrangement of bones and bumps must go through,
and that big ear too, till they learn what to do and hear.
People don't perch like something seen in a zoo
or in tropical sections of Florida. They'll have to buy her
a cheap violin if she wants to make scraping noises.
She is eight years old. What in the world could she wear
that would cover her hinges and disproportions? Her face is
pointed and blank, the brows as light as the hair.

"Mother, is love God's hobby?" At eight you don't even
look up from your scab when you ask it. A kid's squeak,
is that a fit instrument for such a question?
Eight times the seasons turned and cold snow tricked
the earth to death, and still she hasn't noticed.
Her friend has a mean Dad, a milkman always kicks
at the dog, but by some childish hocus-pocus
she blinks them away. She counts ten and sucks in her cheeks
and the globe moves under the green thumb of an Amateur,
the morning yelp, the crying at recess are gone.
In the freeness of time He gardens, and to His leisure
old stems entrust new leaves all winter long.

Hating is hard work, and the uncaring thought is hard,
but loving is easy, love is that lovely play
that makes us and keeps us? No one answers you. Such absurd
charity of the imagination has shamed us, Emily.
I remember now. Legs shoved you up, you couldn't tell
where the next tooth would fall out or grow in, or what
your own nose would look like next year. Anything was possible.
Then it slowed down, and you had to keep what you got.
When this child's body stretches to the grace of her notion,
and she's tamed and curled, may she be free enough to bring
mind and heart to that serious recreation
where anything is still possible—or almost anything.

II

I have never enjoyed those roadside overlooks from which
you can see the mountains of two states. The view keeps generating
a kind of pure, meaningless exaltation
that I can't find a use for. It drifts away from things.

And it seems to me also that the truckdriver's waste of the world
is sobering. When he rolls round it on a callous of macadam,
think how all those limping puppydogs, girls
thumbing rides under the hot sun, or under the white moon

how all those couples kissing at the side of the road,
bad hills, cat eyes, and horses asleep on their feet
must run together into a statement so abstract
that it's tiresome. Nothing in particular holds still in it.

Perhaps he does learn that the planet can still support life,
though with some difficulty. Or even that there is injustice,
since he rolls round and round and may be able to feel
the slight but measurable wobble of the earth on its axis.

But what I find most useful is the poem. To find some spot
on the surface and then bear down until the skin can't stand
the tension and breaks under it, breaks under that half-demented
"pressure of speech" the psychiatrists saw in Pound

is a discreetness of consumption that I value. Only the poem
is strong enough to make the initial rupture,
at least for me. Its view is simultaneous
discovery and reminiscence. It starts with the creature

and stays there, assuming creation is worth the time
it takes, from the first day down to the last line on the last page.
And I've never seen anything like it for making you think
that to spend your life on such old premises is a privilege.

III

> *Your yen two wol slee me sodenly;*
> *I may the beautee of hem not sustene.*
>> Merciles Beaute

When, in the middle of my life, the earth stalks me
with sticks and stones, I fear its merciless beauty.
This morning a bird woke me with a four-note outcry,
and cried out eighteen times. With the shades down, sleepy
as I was, I recognized his agony.
It resembles ours. With one more heave, the day
sends us a generous orb and lets us see
all sights lost when we lie down finally.

And if, in the middle of her life, some beauty falls on
a girl, who turns under its swarm to astonished woman,
then, into that miraculous buzzing, stung
in the lips and eyes without mercy, strangers may run.
An untended power—I pity her and them.
It is late, late; haste! says the falling moon,
as blinded they stand and smart till the fever's done
and blindly she moves, wearing her furious weapon.

Beauty is merciless and intemperate.
Who, turning this way and that, by day, by night,
still stands in the heart-felt storm of its benefit,
will plead in vain for mercy, or cry, "Put out
the lovely eyes of the world, whose rise and set
move us to death!" And never will temper it,
but against that rage slowly may learn to pit
love and art, which are compassionate.

A KIND OF MUSIC

When consciousness begins to add diversity to its intensity, its value is no longer absolute and inexpressible. The felt variations in its tone are attached to the observed movement of its objects; in these objects its values are embedded. A world loaded with dramatic values may thus arise in imagination; terrible and delightful presences may chase one another across the void; life will be a kind of music made by all the senses together. Many animals probably have this kind of experience.

Santayana, *The Life of Reason*

IRRELEVANCE characterizes the behavior of our puppy.
In the middle of the night he decides that he wants to play,
runs off when he's called, when petted is liable to pee,
cowers at a twig and barks at his shadow or a tree,
grins at intruders and bites us in the leg suddenly.

No justification we humans have been able to see
applies to his actions. While we go by the time of day,
or the rules, or the notion of purpose or consistency,
he follows from moment to moment a sensuous medley
that keeps him both totally subject and totally free.

I'll have to admit, though, we've never been tempted to say
that he jumps up to greet us or puts his head on our knee
or licks us or lies at our feet irrelevantly.
When it comes to loving, we find ourselves forced to agree
all responses are reasons and no reason is necessary.

SENTIMENTAL EDUCATION

The North Wind doth blow
and we shall have snow,
and what will the robin do then, poor thing?
He'll sit in the barn
and keep himself warm
and tuck his head under his wing, poor thing.

IN SUMMERS, graceful as any half-grown bird,
she moved in trees that grew in her own yard,

and flourished there, but on the first schoolday
down dropped her tears with "I hate History!"

Dead kings and children lay in tidy rows
in the dusty cases of their long-agoes.

But other subjects were lively—even Numbers
performed at her penciltip its heady wonders,

and Rhyme and Story made such hearty flames
that one by one they singed off all her plumes.

She came down from trees then, and was ready early
all naked to go into love's hurly-burly.

Now she is grown, and in what winter weathers!
She longs for History, or some such feathers.

One wingful to hide her head would keep her warm—
Or so say the other redbreasts in the barn.

THE GENTLE SNORER

WHEN SUMMER came, we locked up our lives and fled
to the woods in Maine, and pulled up over our heads
a comforter filled with batts of piney dark,
tied with crickets' chirretings and the *bork*
of frogs; we hid in a sleep of strangeness from
the human humdrum.

A pleasant noise the unordered world makes wove
around us. Burrowed, we heard the scud of waves,
wrack of bending branch, or plop of a fish
on his heavy home; the little beasts rummaged the brush.
We dimmed to silence, slipped from the angry pull
of wishes and will.

And then we had a three-weeks cabin guest
who snored; he broke the wilderness of our rest.
As all night long he sipped the succulent air,
that rhythm we shared made visible to the ear
a rich refreshment of the blood. We fed in
unison with him.

A sound we dreamed and woke to, over the snuff
of wind, not loud enough to scare off the roof
the early morning chipmunks. Under our skins
we heard, as after disease, the bright, thin
tick of our time. Sleeping, he mentioned death
and celebrated breath.

He went back home. The water flapped the shore.
A thousand bugs drilled at the darkness. Over
the lake a loon howled. Nothing spoke up for us,
salvagers always of what we have always lost;
and we thought that what the night needed was more of man,
he left us so partisan.

PARATROOPER

FROM the dark side, feet first, breech birth, the fighter falls
and this babe is small among perihelions
and his first breath crawls like a worm through impersonal countries
of no sins, but so many instinctive and unsatisfying suns.

And he falls like a scream from the nipple stars that stipple his passage
while with hands of wind and fear his body is bathed to the bone.
He tumbles and turns and yearns for a sign from the presences
who hurry in orbits beside him, unsmiling, adult, and not known.

What world is his, orphan that he is, in voids and valences
with cries that leave no answer in an enormous room—
Whose loss is his, no brother's or lover's, as wild he runs
through shadowed streets, and knocks at doors where no one is at
    home—

So fast and fierce he falls, and in vain he calls to the mother
for peace from the speed of his passage, the fire of his falling that
    blinds him
but his will flies out like an angered bird to peck at the foe
and memory, strongest myth, like a strange moth, opens behind him.

And now his course is slowed, his shoulders heavy now.
With the pull of angels-up and devils-down he is weak.
He feels the shame when the flu came when he was a little boy
and asafoetida, like an albatross, hung on his neck.

And now idea, pure unicorn in the air, he is riding
and the skies are hung, stars down, with crystalline streets of word
and zero, the daemon that tormented him in school, is calling
but on his hand drops down the ripe, real dung of a bird.

And what of love, lost leaf, will he be finding now
like stray dogs that stopped to lick his hand and then ran on,
and what of hate, white heat, will he be feeling now
like the time the strange man kissed his mother when his father was

    out of town?

And is luck, bright rock on a string, strung safely around his neck
  now?
for he broke the wishbone at the home of his friend and got his
  hardball.
And is loss, black bird with the blooded beak, perched on his
  shoulder?
for the penny rolled away from his fingers and fell in a dark well.

But, see, the clouds roll back, some heavy homeland is shining.
In ascension, slow and silent, he goes to it in peace
and all the while white shadow, alter ego, follows after him
and he breaks through the membrane of history and sees the trees.

The thunder rises like mist and the leaves like lovers enfold him
and time, rocks, rooks and roses grow from his body, O blossomer, he.
And now he bends his knees and the delicate bones of his feet
strike earth, his short-haired, hell and heaven hard, maturity.

DEATH BY AESTHETICS

HERE IS the doctor, an abstracted lover,
dressed as a virgin, coming to keep the tryst.
The patient was early; she is lovely; but yet
she is sick, his instruments will agree on this.

Is this the place, she wonders, and is he the one?
Yes, love is the healer, he will strip her bare,
and all his machinery of definition
tells her experience is costly here,

so she is reassured. The doctor approaches
and bends to her heart. But she sees him sprout like a tree
with metallic twigs on his fingers and blooms of chrome
at his eye and ear for the sterile ceremony.

Oh tight and tighter his rubber squeeze of her arm.
"Ahhh" she sighs at a chilly touch on her tongue.
Up the tubes her breath comes crying, as over her,
back and breast, he moves his silver thumb.

His fluoroscope hugs her. Soft the intemperate girl,
disordered. Willing she lies while he unfolds
her disease, but a stem of glass protects his fingertips
from her heat, nor will he catch her cold.

He peels her. Under the swaddling epiderm
her body is the same blue bush. Beautiful canals
course like a postcard scene that's sent him often.
He counts the *tiptup, tiptup* of her dutiful valves.

Pain hides like a sinner in her mesh of nerves.
But her symptoms constellate! Quickly he warms
to his consummation, while her fever flares
in its wick of vein, her wicked blood burns.

He hands her a paper. "Goodbye. Live quietly,
make some new friends. I've seen these stubborn cases
cured with time. My bill will arrive. Dear lady,
it's been a most enjoyable diagnosis."

She clings, but her fingers slip on his starchy dress.
"Don't leave me! Learn me! If this is all, you've swindled
my whole booty of meaning, where is my dearness?
Pore against pore, the delicate hairs commingled,

with cells and ligaments, tissue lapped on bone,
meet me, feel the way my body feels,
and in my bounty of dews, fluxes and seasons,
orifices, in my wastes and smells

see self. Self in the secret stones I chafed
to shape in my bladder. Out of a dream I fished
the ache that feeds in my stomach's weedy slough.
This tender swelling's the bud of my frosted wish.

Search out my mind's embroidery of scars.
My ichor runs to death so speedily,
spit up your text and taste my living texture.
Sweat to hunt me with love, and burn with me."

But he is gone. "Don't touch me," was all he answered.
"Separateness," says the paper. The world, we beg,
will keep her though she's caught its throbbing senses,
its bugs still swim in her breath, she's bright with its plague.

A RELATIVE AND AN ABSOLUTE

*"It has been cool so far for December, but of course the cold doesn't
last long down here. The Bible is being fulfilled so rapidly that it
looks like it won't be long until Jesus will come in the air, with a
shout, and all those who have accepted Jesus as their own personal
Saviour will be caught up to meet him and then that terrible war
will be on earth. The battle of Armageddon. And all the unsaved
people will have to go through the great tribulation. Hope you are
both well. Bye."*

AN AUNT, my down-to-earth father's sibling, went to stay
in Texas, and had to continue by mail, still thanklessly,
her spiritual supervision of the family.

Texas orchards are fruitful. A card that would portray
this fact in green and orange, and even more colorfully say
on its back that Doom is nearly upon us, came regularly

at birthday, Easter and Christmas—and sometimes between the
three.
That the days passed, and the years, never bothered her prophecy;
she restressed, renewed and remailed its imminence faithfully.

Most preaching was wrong, she felt, but found for her kin on
Sunday,
in one voice on one radio station, one truth for all to obey.
Salvation being thus limited, it seemed to me

there was something unpleasant about that calm tenacity
of belief that so many others would suffer catastrophe
at any moment. She seemed too smug a protégée.

Otherwise, I rather liked her. Exchanging a recipe
or comparing winters with neighbors, she took life quietly
in a stuffy bungalow, among doilies of tatting and crochet.

She had married late, and enjoyed the chance to baby
a husband, to simmer the wholesome vegetables and see
that vitamins squeezed from his fruit were drunk without delay.

11

Though she warned of cities and churches and germs, some modesty
or decorum, when face to face with us, wouldn't let her convey
her vision of Armageddon. But the postcards set it free.

It was hovering over the orange groves, she need only lay
her sewing aside, and the grandeur and rhythm of its poetry
came down and poured in her ear, her pencil moved eloquently.

She wrote it and wrote it. She will be "caught up," set free from her
    clay
as Christ comes "with a shout in the air" and trumpeting angels play,
and "the terrible war will be on earth" on that Judgment Day,

expecting all those years her extinction of body would be
attended by every creature, wrapped round in the tragedy
of the world, in its pandemonium and ecstasy.

When she died last winter, several relatives wrote to say
a kidney stone "as big as a peach pit" took her away.
Reading the letters, I thought, first of all, of the irony,

then, that I myself, though prepared to a certain degree,
will undoubtedly feel, when I lie there, as lonesome in death as she
and just as surprised at its trivial, domestic imagery.

TOWARD A DEFINITION OF MARRIAGE

I

IT IS to make a fill, not find a land.
Elsewhere, often, one sights americas of awareness,
suddenly there they are, natural and anarchic,
with plantings scattered but rich, powers to be harnessed—
but this is more like building a World's Fair island.
Somebody thought it could be done, contracts are signed,
and now all materials are useful, everything; sludge
is scooped up and mixed with tin cans and fruit rinds,
even tomato pulp and lettuce leaves are solid
under pressure. Presently the ground humps up and shows.
But this marvel of engineering is not all.
A hodgepodge of creatures (no bestiary would suppose
such an improbable society) are at this time
turned loose to run on it, first shyly, then more free,
and must keep, for self's sake, wiles, anger, much of their
spiney or warted nature, yet learn courtesy.

II

It is closest to picaresque, but essentially artless.
If there were any experts, they are dead, it takes too long.
How could its structure be more than improvising,
when it never ends, but line after line plods on,
and none of the ho hum passages can be skipped?
It has a bulky knowledge, but what symbol comes anywhere near
suggesting it? No, the notion of art won't fit it—
unless—when it's embodied. For digression there
is meaningful, and takes such joy in the slopes and crannies
that every bony gesture is generous, full,
all lacy with veins and nerves. There, the spirit
smiles in its skin, and impassions and sweetens to style.
So this comes to resemble a poem found in his notebooks
after the master died. A charred, balky man, yet one day
as he worked at one of those monuments, the sun guiled him,
and he turned to a fresh page and simply let play
his great gift on a small ground. Yellowed, unpublished,
he might have forgotten he wrote it. (All this is surmise.)
But it's known by heart now; it rounded the steeliest shape
to shapeliness, it was so loving an exercise.

13

III

Or, think of it as a duel of amateurs.
These two have almost forgot how it started—in an alley,
impromptu, and with a real affront. One thought,
"He is not me," and one, "She is not me,"
and they were coming toward each other with sharp knives
when someone saw it was illegal, dragged them away,
bundled them into some curious canvas clothing,
and brought them to this gym that is almost dark, and empty.
Now, too close together for the length of the foils,
wet with fear, they dodge, stumble, strike,
and if either finally thinks he would rather be touched
than touch, he still must listen to the clang and tick
of his own compulsive parrying. Endless. Nothing
but a scream for help can make the authorities come.
If it ever turns into more of a dance than a duel,
it is only because, feeling more skillful, one
or the other steps back with some notion of grace
and looks at his partner. Then he is able to find
not a wire mask for his target, but a red heart
sewn on the breast like a simple valentine.

IV

If there's a Barnum way to show it, then think back
to a climax in the main tent. At the foot of the bleachers, a road
encloses the ringed acts; consider that as its design,
and consider whoever undertakes it as the whole parade
which, either as preview or summary, assures the public
hanging in hopeful suspense between balloons and peanutshells
that it's all worthwhile. The ponies never imagined
anything but this slow trot of ribbons and jinglebells.
An enormous usefulness constrains the leathery bulls
as they stomp on, and hardly ever run amuck.
The acrobats practiced all their lives for this easy
contortion, and clowns are enacting a necessary joke
by harmless zigzags in and out of line.
But if the procession includes others less trustworthy?

When they first see the circle they think some ignorant
cartographer has blundered. The route is a lie,
drawn to be strict but full, drawn so each going forth
returns, returns to a more informed beginning.
And still a familiar movement might tempt them to try it,
but since what they know is not mentioned in the tromboning
of the march, neither the day-long pace of caged
impulse, nor the hurtle of night's terrible box-cars,
they shrink in their stripes and refuse; other performers
drive them out and around with whips and chairs.
They never tame, but may be taught to endure
the illusion of tameness. Year after year their paws
pad out the false curve, and their reluctant parading
extends the ritual's claim to its applause.

V

Say, for once, that the start is a pure vision
like the blind man's (though he couldn't keep it, trees
soon bleached to familiar) when the bandage came off
and what a world could be first fell on his eyes.
Say it's when campaigns are closest to home
that farsighted lawmakers oftenest lose their way.
And repeat what everyone knows and nobody wants
to remember, that always, always expediency
must freckle the fairest wishes. Say, when documents,
stiff with history, go right into the council chambers
and are rolled up to shake under noses, are constantly read from,
or pounded on, or passed around, the parchment limbers;
and, still later, if these old papers are still being shuffled,
commas will be missing, ashes will disfigure a word;
finally thumbprints will grease out whole phrases, the clear prose
won't mean much; it can never be wholly restored.
Curators mourn the perfect idea, for it crippled
outside of its case. Announce that at least it can move
in the imperfect action, beyond the windy oratory,
of marriage, which is the politics of love.

II. A TIME OF
BEES

ELEMENTARY ATTITUDES

I. Earth

ALL SPRING the birds walked on this wormy world.
Now they avoid the ground, lining up on limbs
and fences, beaks held open, panting. And behold,
in a romper suit and tap shoes, my neighbor comes

click, click, past the gawking birds to her patio.
A middle-aged woman—they've known her for months, as have I,
coming down the side walk in a housedress twice a day
to throw them breadcrumbs and talk over the fence to me

as I weed and plant or write poems in the backyard garden.
Now I am dazzled by the flowers and by my neighbor in rompers.
She says it's hot, so hot, her house is like an oven.
Aren't the flowers bright, she says. They are worse

than bright these days, it seems to me, they are burning,
blazing in red salvia and orange daylilies,
in marigolds, in geraniums—even the petunias are turning
violent. Rose, red, orange, cerise,

yellow flame together and spread over their borders.
The earth and my diligent gardening, what have we done
to my neighbor? Arms wide out, she suddenly flutters
up into the air and comes down, and leaps again,

and clickety-clickety-clickety *rat-a-tat-tat,*
all over her patio she goes in a frenzy of tapdancing.
What new July conflagration is this, and what
would her husband say, who works in a drugstore? In the spring

she admired my jonquils and, later, the peonies calmly,
tossing bread to the birds as she chatted. They grew tamer and tamer.
Now they are squeaking and wheeling away from what they see,
and I am making good resolutions for next summer:

This collaboration with the earth should be done with care.
Even gardens, it seems, can set off explosions, and so
I'll have blue salvia and blue ageratum next year,
pale petunias, more poems, and some plumbago.

II. Air

My primitive attitude toward the air makes it impossible
to be anything but provincial. I'll never climb Eiffels,
see Noh plays, big game, leprous beggars, implausible
rites, all in one lifetime. My friends think it's awful.

It leads to overcompensation: in the kitchen, prunes
in the potroast, kidneys in the wine and the restrained misery
of a hamburger-loving husband; in the yard, prone
plants from far places that never adjusted to Missouri;

in the mind, an unreasoning dislike of haiku, and in least
appropriate gatherings, innocent plans for the remission
of the world's woes—"Well, why don't we all just . . . ?"
People blush for me in political discussion.

It leads also, when visiting friends in California or reading
at the YMHA, to spending three-fourths of the time
on the way and only one-fourth of it there, and to travelling
always in the company of beginners. When I leave home

I ride with farm couples bringing the granddaughter back
for a visit, boys going off to their first big city,
honeymooners, college kids, toddlers who might get airsick,
and Texans who hire a whole car to get drunk cross-country.

Sooner or later most of these graduate to planes,
while I start out all over again on the ground.
The Texans and I are stuck with our beginnings.
To get a panoramic view of my own home town

I once took a helicopter ride and found everything unreal—
my house, lost in that vista half a mile under,
and whoever was grieving up there in a glass bubble,
pretending to enjoy the sights and growing blinder and blinder.

I can stand an outside view of myself, but nothing
about a bird's-eye view elevates or animates me in the slightest.
Maybe people who don't like air should just stop breathing.
I breathe, but I tend toward asthma and bronchitis.

III. Fire

When feathers and fur came off, and the skin
bared, then we became open
to all manifestations of fire, to the sun's

inconceivable consummations. And I
was born in the busy-ness of that great day
of heat and light, hunting with my whole body.

The blood boils. "A higher temperature,
by hastening the chemical reactions of the creature,
allows it to live more quickly and more

intensely." Biologists are in favor of burning,
and I too, creature singeing
to certain death in the metabolic blessing,

I too celebrate my fires. In Maine
the treetops came sizzling down and I ran
with chipmunks and foxes. Utterances, mean

or stealthy or rhymed, charged, live,
fall all day on the tindery nerves.
These ignitions, and those in the stove

of my flesh, underhand, and speculations,
and barbecue and fireplace in their seasons
keep me quick. Cigarettes blazon

me to words, and bourbon. Some eyes
are best sparks. Our stuff multiplies
in warmth, we are lovers from the first ceremonies

of protein, the lonesome cold stars
miss us. A first breath, and our natures
are afire, we run in the blistering years.

IV. Water

It is hard to remember what one is mostly made of.
Floating on top, as ark, is a sort of sieve
carrying my wet brain, and under the waves
ovaries and liver and other items sway
like the bulbs and stems of some aquatic lily.

But even here, at the confluence of the Missouri
and the Mississippi, late summers are dry
and there is little snow in winter. Abstractions are the key
to being. Scientists flourish, but swimmers
are bitten to death by catfish in these rivers.

When I landed, out of the broken bag of my mother,
heat and buoyancy had to be learned all over,
but there are few such dangerous floods, so far.
On humid days, under a green sea of oak leaves,
I move secretly, like a skin-diver, but don't dive.

The mind is seldom wholly immersed. We live
willingly, fear both drouth and drowning, conceive
in swampy places, and drink to provoke love.
When love's unkindness punctures the eyeball, tears
remind us again that we are made of water.

A SERIOUS CASE

"The [life of] the democratic man . . is motley and manifold and . . this distracted existence he terms . . freedom."
"The perfect guardian of our State must be a philosopher . . he whose mind is fixed on true being."
"It will be our duty to select . . natures which are fitted for the task of [protecting] our City . . quick to see and swift to overtake the enemy."
"Carpenters and smiths and many other artisans will be sharers in our little State . . and salesmen . . hunters . . servants . . tutors . . nurses . . barbers . . cooks."
"The artist . . knows nothing of true existence . . Let this be our defence for sending [him] away . . for the safety of the City."

IF WE happen to choke up on history, none too soon
we resort to "The Republic." A receptionist lets us in
at the door we're driven to, on acres of sedative green
or the city's edge. Let theory save us, if it can.

When all the white rats in the world have confirmed our flaws,
and the separateness of our wish, or its treaty with laws
where either night causes day or there is no cause
is cramped in a formula every bright youngster knows,

we'll see what we'll see. In the meantime, Plato will do
for rest in a dream some two thousand years ago.
White-coated experts have classified us, and now
the door whispers shut, whatever is here is true.

Top floor, Ward Three: Exalted thinkers roam
and bump harmlessly into abstractions outside their own
abstraction. With each, disguised out of deference to brain,
is his earthly form, sacked in a rough white gown

over rough white pajamas. Here every head has to make
an experiment that might startle even the smart Greek—
to design a New Order, yes, but then bring it the whole meek
self as citizen, and try out how it will work.

Habit, the human stance, inviolateness of symbol,
the universal fable of appearance—all fail
under such a ferocious demand that truth out and time tell.
A. paces off life's length from wall to wall.

B., in a quiet corner, concealed by her hair
thrown over her face, has bombed the earth for an hour,
but will glue it together again, this time in a square.
C. points at sinful God sneaking under a chair.

D. is led out and shut up. Alas, he found
neither justice nor mercy would function in his State of Mind,
and his torment's too loud. E., on his knees, is enthroned.
F. tightens his logic, and notes how the windowblind,

the cup of milk, a black playing card and a word
confirm his premises. (But, sorry for such absurd
and total commitment, observers are fighting it hard;
they stun these out after a while, and restock the ward.)

Middle floor, Ward Two: Brought away from his barracks, his aim,
his practice maneuvers, locked in a living room,
is the man of action whose dedication is grim
and steadfast—to find the foul enemy and destroy him.

Held together, all agree that delay is despair
although nothing has ever defined the foe but the mirror.
With pills and injections, bars at the window and door,
propagandists persuade them to wait, there is no war.

But they cling to their girding for battle—crumpled clothes,
loose shoelaces, straggly hair. As a calming ruse,
all calls to duty are silenced, yet often at agonized
attention they slump, with bent head and cast-down eyes.

The Ideal encloses them neatly. What else would condone
such transcendent ardor? Each follows orders within
himself. Each is the hero who will act alone.
Even when disarmed, with nailfiles, neckties, pins,

deodorants and belts removed, J. will pick at his face,
K., who is clever and devious, for weeks will refuse
or vomit his food, L. weeps at the pacifist disgrace
of her breathing, while M. tries cheer as a trick for release.

Quiet till now in his forced retreat, N. suddenly
cries "Help!" at the window. He's watched. Twice more, and they'll see
that he's turned philosopher, has to be sent to Ward Three.
(But this kind of misfortune could happen in any army.)

First floor, Ward One: The populace mills all over,
layers of the daily groundwork, tireless re-weavers
of meaning by repetition, tunnellers by clever
hands and wits in the trivia of human endeavor.

But seldom outside do we see such dramatically pure
representatives. Each is an all too genuine character,
and one domestic virtue or vice is made clear
through the action of each, as in children's literature.

Q. is HELPFUL—all day will chat, will roll
R.'s hair into pincurls, wind up a skein of wool
for S., sew a button on T.; (but in the dark lull
of night lies hunting, can find no friends at all).

(Though she kept to her room at home,) SHY R. now and then
will accept U.'s (trembling) offer of a magazine—
he is NERVOUS. X., who is FEARFUL (of pigeons and men)
smiles at a crooner held back by the TV screen.

S., the CRITICAL, knits. But the yarn is too coarse
and too green, the room too warm. Yesterday was worse,
chilly, with spotted lettuce at lunch, squeaky doors.
(Her sensitive skin breaks out at all things, their perverse

imperfection.) No one's as HAPPY as T. The wreck
of a lifetime, in fact the whole ridiculous mistake
of being, makes him laugh out loud. (But employers will seek
a humor more business-like, a more practical joke.)

V.'s INDECISIVE (and mornings for him are hell—
which sock should he put on first?) Afternoons he does well,
plays pingpong with W. (who tests his own motives until
he faints in the evenings), being CONSCIENTIOUS. The smell

of X.'s perfume, her heeltaps, her satin swish
announce she is VAIN. (Three husbands have left her, she's rushed
to death, screams Stop! Stop! at the dizzying push
of wrinkles in loneliness.) Y.'s perpetual blush

only means that she's ANXIOUS. (Her face is hot but sweat
trickles cold on her leg, for the worst hasn't happened yet.)
Z.—but this ward is jammed. Even sampling it
takes far too long, and we've run out of alphabet.

Well, our scholarly sojourn is over. We must go.
We'll pay, of course, for the privilege of saying goodbye
to past ideas. Electricity, chemistry, industry,
understanding, love and time all took us away

from the classic Statesman. A hard democracy
reinstates us. It yields to the flow of Becoming freely
and moves with that aimless mixture of water and debris,
but its manner of movement aims at the possibility

that home-made restrictions may heal the lunatic will
and that heart and mind, though classless, may be schooled well
by each other. Boatless and untherapeutic, its control
neither supports nor simplifies the individual,

who becomes, in a fluid condition of rule and river,
all wards in one, the dreamer, the doer and the lover
of life's detail. He becomes, in fact, a survivor
of the kind Plato banished, knowing he would scramble all over

and scuttle the Ark. To swim, mixing grace with reason,
interfering with form for the sake of personal motion
and working with constant depth in the currents of season
is his stately duty; to sink, his forgiveable treason.

RECOVERY

I. The Dormitory

IN MEXICO the little mixed herds come home in the evening,
slow through that hard-colored landscape, all driven together—
the hens, a few pigs, a burro, two cows, and the thin
perro that is everywhere. It is the same scene here.

The nurses herd us. In our snouts and feathers
we move through the rigid cactus shapes of chairs
colored to lie, belie terror and worse.
Assorted and unlikely as the lives we bear,

we go together to bed, one dozen of us.
It was a hard day's grazing, we fed on spines of courtesy
and scratched up a few dry bugs of kindness.
But we deserved less than that generosity.

Our teats of giving hang dry. Our poor peons are bewildered
and poorer still, the whole landscape is impoverished
by the unnatural economy of this group's greed,
whose bark is bitter, who are swaybacked, fruitless, unfleshed.

The pen echoes to a meaningless moo, "I want to go home,"
one cackles over sins, one yaps in rhythmic complaining,
but those shapes under the sheets are not like mine.
We are locked in unlove. I am sick of my own braying.

The metaphor shakes like my hand. Come, Prince of Pills,
electric kiss, undo us, and we will appear
wearing each other's pain like silk, the awful
richness of feeling we blame, but barely remember.

II. The Doctors

Those who come from outside are truly foreign.
How are we to believe in the clear-eyed and clean-shaven?
The jungle I crawl through on my hands and knees,
the whole monstrous ferny land of my own nerves,
hisses and quakes at these upright missionaries
wearing immaculate coats, and will not open.

25

Mine is waiting outside like a mild boy.
He is unarmed, he will never make it to this anarchy.
Somewhere down his civil streams, through his system,
a survivor came babbling, half-wild from stink and sun,
and news leaked out about our savage customs.
I bit my bloody heart again today.

At night I dream of tables and chairs, beds,
hospitals. I wake. I am up to my waist in mud.
Everything shrieks, cloudbursts of confusion are beating
on my head as I twist and grab for vines, sweating
to make a raft, to tie something together. He is waiting.
I want his words after all, those cheap beads.

Stranger, forgive me, I have clawed as close as I can.
Your trinkets clink to the ground, it is all dark
on the other side of my impenetrable network.
I will wallow and gnaw—but wait, you are coming back,
and at touch, flamethrower, underbrush goes down.
Now I can stand by you, fellow-citizen.

III. A Memory

"Write a letter to Grandpa," my mother said, but he smelled old.
"He'll give you something nice," she said, but I was afraid.
He never looked at me, he muttered to himself, and he hid
bad things to drink all over his house, and Grandma cried.
A gray stranger with a yellowed mustache, why should I have mailed
my very first message to him? Well, consider the innocent need
that harries us all: "Your Aunt Callie thinks she's smart, but *her* kid
never sent her first letter to Pa." (To hold her I had to be good.)
"You've learned to write. Write Grandpa!" she said, so I did.

It was hard work. "Dear Grandpa, How are you, I am fine,"
but I couldn't come to the the end of a word when I came to the
    margin,
and the lines weren't straight on the page. I erased that paper so thin
you could almost see through it in spots. I couldn't seem to learn
to look ahead. (Mother, remember we both had to win.)

"We are coming to visit you next Sunday if it does not rain.
Yours truly, your loving granddaughter, Mona Van Duyn."
That Sunday he took me aside and gave me the biggest coin
I ever had, and I ran away from the old man.

"Look, Mother, what Grandpa gave me. And as soon as I get back
    home
I'll write him again for another half dollar." But Mother said
    "Shame!"
and so I was ashamed. But I think at that stage of the game,
or any stage of the game, things are almost what they seem
and the exchange was fair. Later in the afternoon I caught him.
"Medicine," he said, but he must have known his chances were slim.
People don't hide behind the big fern, I wasn't dumb,
and I was Grandma's girl. "So, *Liebling,* don't tell them,"
he said, but that sneaky smile called me by my real name.

Complicity I understood. What human twig isn't bent
by the hidden weight of its wish for some strict covenant?
"Are you going to tell?" he wanted to know, and I said, "No, I won't."
He looked right at me and straightened his mouth and said, "So, *Kind,*
we fool them yet," and it seemed to me I knew what he meant.
Then he reached in his pocket and pulled out two candies covered
    with lint,
and we stood there and each sucked one. *"Ja,* us two, we know what
    we want."
When he leaned down to chuck my chin I caught my first Grandpa-
    scent.
Oh, it was a sweet seduction on pillows of peppermint!

And now, in the middle of life, I'd like to learn how to forgive
the heart's grandpa, mother and kid, the hard ways we have to love.

IV. By the Pond in the Park, by the Hospital

The grass is green, the trees and the bench are green.
Parked cars, like aquarium pebbles, circle the pond.
A roar, a dry sprinkle, and a good machine
goes by, cutting grass in a ten-foot strip. In the wind
walk blackbirds. This is the closest I've ever been
to an elegant, high-stepping one. He is watching my hand
and I, watching his red and yellow wing, am sane.

Little dandy, your chemistry, and not your fine
feather, dazzles my half-familiar head,
for, three blocks back, marvelous returns are routine
and the simple map to decay unreadable, or unread.
—To trust perception again is like learning to lean
on water. The water, moving over minnows, is haunted.
Dandelions bloom, the trees and the grass are green.

In the hospital, other matters go on, the obscene
writhing of feelings like worms on hooks, and all mute,
all smelling of wild loss; and now the mowing man
stops and dismounts, throws something in the pond, something light,
then starts up his motors—an empty coffee tin
that scares the minnows away, sinking in the rot
of leaves, to the bottom. That inundation was a dream.

All around the pond a bracelet of cars is curled
and the wind smells green through the mower's unerring noise.
I think through my senses, I chew grass, and a squirrel
chews too, but something hard. Melodrama never has
real answers. Memory will come, like some quiet girl,
slow-spoken and friendly, to tell me whatever it was
I knew I wanted in this grassy world.

AN ESSAY ON CRITICISM

STANDING in the kitchen, ready to rip open the tinfoil,
I paused to appreciate how abstraction flatters my will,

how efficiently it takes out of time the qualities I can use
and rejects the others. Assuming onion soup as my purpose,

the onions in my cupboard, which used to be, so to speak, real,
insisted on their whole nature, were never so sweetly under control—

they were always inconveniently rotting or trying to bloom
or spraying my eyes with perverse misdirection of their perfume,

while these neat and peaceful little particles will go into the steam,
inoffensive to my notions of what an onion or a tear humanly means,

and come simmering back to what might be called onions again,
or stay on the shelf, drily possible, inert until I need them.

I had paused with the package, as I say, but at the doorbell's ring
I went and let in a friend whose radiance was transforming.

"Let me tell you this minute!" she cried, and just inside the door
clutched at my sleeve and held me to her eloquence like the Mariner.

"His name doesn't matter—he won't know—for my future he is no
    one—
but I know now—I've learned what love is—how love is like a
    poem—

how it 'makes nothing happen,' how it 'lies in the valley of its saying,'
how it lives by its tensions with the roundness and perfection of a
    daydream,

how it delights in itself, doubles back on itself, is 'to be'
in the full awareness of its being, its own elegance of play,

is an equilibrium of sound, sight and sense all together
springing to vehement life and celebrating each other,

how it finds what it wants from reality and makes up the rest,
but is finally its own reference, exists in its own interest,

how it kindles the world that is made, the lie that has made it,
the mind's grasp, the heart's hold, the senses' rich hauls of the scoop-
    net,

and while passion, which is only its paraphrase, dies of quick pleasure,
it survives in its difficult wholeness, its ceremonious self-enclosure,

beyond sincerity, an exclusive configuration
that includes me in art, lets me say, 'This is *my* creation!'

Oh, I'm only an amateur," she said, a young woman and poet,
"but you know all about it," to me, enough older to deny it,

and she stopped and waited, and I stood like a rebellious nun
whose habit is read too simply in the sense of separation.

Beginners have ignorance as their danger and precious privilege,
but re-beginners suffer and fail through distrust of knowledge.

Yet I looked, out of vanity, for an honest advisory role
and turned up a lack of innocence, at least, that might be helpful;

for, once one has trembled through an eavesdrop on private con-
    fession,
one writes to Dear Someone Somewhere, assuming mutual indiscre-
    tion.

"You're published now," I told her, "in your eyes, your whole air,
so your poem is half of the truth, the other half is the reader.

All you've described, that enchanted, self-created 'self-enclosure,'
is made to lie in print in an enchanting self-exposure

to the one who, having by accident or inquisitiveness
turned to its page, puts all his perception at its service,

by understanding goes on past its artful shyness
to its artful appeal, and through that to its real fineness,

'suspends disbelief' that its loving selection is total,
forgets what it doesn't mention, the dust on the windowsill,

the office routine, any routine, and . . . beholds.
Later, of course, come tests more critically controlled,

but a poem, believe me, by consent, never by coercion,
slowly, deeply, seriously can move another person,

for, although the instant of judgment it starts from is spontaneous,
unwilled, the rest of its painful and painstaking fuss

results from the pressure of a passionately serious wish
on invention which would rather be carefree, playful, coltish—

the 'wish to be believed.' A poem exerts an intention
of passing all tests, of standing as permanent intervention

between reader and reader-as-he-was. I just mean," I ended,
"being written and published, something is somehow being said."

She thanked me, looking somewhat thoughtful, and said goodbye, and
    left,
and I gripped in turn, from long practice, a theoretical Wedding
    Guest,

confessing to someone less starry-eyed than she about engagements
how the belief that to be believed is always of consequence

comes to hang on the pencil, heavy, and how merely growing old
makes all moving weightier and more expensive—time favors the
    household—

yet a poem's way of happening won't let anything happen at all
unless it is serious—it is no brothel and has no windfalls;

and how, though it's not for its own sake, pure revel in its own nature,
it must keep its salutation secret and be written as if it were,

expressing the contradiction that only this professional lie
permits the collaboration that can make it come true;

and how a reader who comes to take in the surprise of each pathway
in a world of formal difference and difference of personality

may find other surprises. (There is one, impressed as trailbreaker,
who returns to the poem as a kind of conscientious marriage-broker

and raps it and taps it and maps it clear back to a region
where the writer stands shivering in the art as artless human

and takes down her measurements—but we needn't worry about him;
he bundled up for the chill, reached that climate as professional
  pilgrim.)

But there's one who goes back to his business so provoked by the tour
he denounces the vacation, swears he won't take it any more,

but on the way to the office finds he is walking to its rhythm
and changes his stride, but its rhyme goes bing-bong in his bosom,

tries TV at night, but its imagery covers his screen,
and closes his eyes but his memory insists on its meaning,

and finds that it is modifying the dust on his windowsill
and its sum is including parts much greater than its whole,

until, willing to do something, he makes an apprehensive return
and runs through the foreign scenery, feeling strangely at home

(for what other world is there but the one we believe to be,
that we touch and are touched by in affections, conceptions and
  body?),

till he reaches an ultimate region and sees, standing there,
himself and the writer, two humans, artless and similar—

a likeness proved out of difference—and, enlightened in its sunshine,
he sees they've been caring about each other the whole time,

and so, through its other active agent, the poem is a power,
and the responsibility . . .

                    but it was almost time for dinner.

All of a sudden, when I went back into the kitchen,
tears came to my eyes, galvanized by a sort of pain.

Now of course I remember perfectly all that was going on
at the start, but it wasn't leading to empathy with the onion.

The inner life of that bulb would never come to interest me;
I am not like an onion, I don't wish anyone else to be.

I was only using the onion. It is only useful,
and, defining it by so few qualities, I make it immortal

and agree with the science of onions that all onions are the same
and don't see what is individual. I don't have time.

Was the pang for poetry? I meant to take time for that,
for what is gentle, idealistic and fair and, in the long run, right.

I wasn't just using poetry. I was caring about it.
I believe life wouldn't be nearly so meaningful without it.

I want them illuminating each other as much as possible,
and in the foregoing, whenever their likeness grew implausible,

whenever the see-saw poise of the metaphor weakened,
I held up the poem's side first, and life's side second,

for I believe in art's process of working through otherness to recognition
and in its power that comes from acceptance, and not imposition—

for people, that is; and if life is not a poem, and this is clear,
one can still imply that one sometimes wishes it were.

As I emptied out the tinfoil package, tears fell in the pot
as if onionjuice had caused them; the important thing is, it had not.

Let technology salt the soup, let it remove every eye-sting
that has no necessitous human predicament as its meaning.

These tears can season only if they fall on a shoulder
and a breathing, feeling recipient responds to their moisture,

but poetry didn't cause them either. The pain, that tearjerk,
was life, asserting its primacy in a well-timed rebuke,

and the assertion is valid. A poem can stay formally seated
till its person-to-person call, centuries later, is completed,

being abstract enough to afford inertness on the shelf
and yet being the self's own lifelike abstraction of itself.

But these tears, I remind, well and fall in a room with a clock.
Out of action they come, into action they intend to hurry back.

Their message is more vital than their grace can be, and when they
    speak
they adopt with justice the imperfect urgency of rhetoric,

basing their case on unearned, inglorious similarity:
"Dear reader, there is nothing immortal about the you and the me.

We must move in time, time moves, we must care right away!"
Less beautifully patient than a poem, one might call them an essay.

POT-AU-FEU

*Everything that is going on in Nature . . . increase[s] the entropy of
the part of the world where it is going on. A living organism . . .
tends to approach the state of maximum entropy, which is death. It
is continually sucking orderliness from its environment [and] free-
ing itself from all the entropy it cannot help producing . . . [and]
thus it evades the decay to thermodynamical equilibrium.*
Schrödinger, What is Life?

*I remembered how Mrs. Procter once said to me that, having had a
long life of many troubles, sufferings, encumbrances and devasta-
tions, it was, in the evening of that life, a singular pleasure, a deeply
felt luxury, to her, to* sit and read a book: *the mere sense of the
security of it, the sense that, with all she had outlived,* nothing could
now happen, *was so great within her.*
Henry James, Notebooks

IT IS all too clear that order wasn't our invention.
What we thought we imposed on Nature was her own intention,
and if anyone doubts it, let's see who's the steady old hand
at doting arrangement, her metabolism or our mind:
Watch her anticipate our cellular howl
by spooning out stable linkings of chemical gruel,
or, using the disorder that is death to us,
producing more anchovies and asparagus,
or, for our snacks, slicing up without pause or limit
a million billion other lives a minute.

But, lo, in the high society of consciousness,
we diet to death on our own affectional fuss,
rocking the environment through disordering lips
with the erratic heat motion of our relationships,
turning living to losing, burning with need for our fellow
and filling the air with exhaust for him to swallow;
for to feed on trouble and void a composed overhaul
takes a structure humbler than man's, and more Natural.
Yet since mind and body are under each other's thumb
and you come to my mind, something really ought to be done.

You'll have to admit, my darling, that we tire each other,
exhaling such smogs of entropy that the weather
is unwholesome here for us in our weakened condition.
Already we're worn from testing an important mutation

35

of the internal scene, and we've used lots of heat to start
taking off on those dizzying quantum jumps of the heart,
yet we're forced to keep on regenerating the nicks
of a thousand daily empathic enzyme kicks,
and to carry, wherever we go in our hungry waning,
the sweet encumbrance of one another's meaning.

And so, to balance the emotional wear-and-tear,
let me set a table in the atmosphere.
They say if a glassful of marked molecules were poured
in the Seven Seas, and diligently stirred,
then in any glassful dipped from any ocean
you'd find one hundred out of the original potion.
I can't prove a poem's caloric count is so high,
nor know my particular measuring will reach your eye,
but I'll pour by faith, and believe that wherever you sup
the nourishing orderliness has been thickened up.

The move is mine, my sex is less prone to the torment
of organic dignity, and more attached to our ferment.
I'll debase my system, I'll eat like a weed, and exchange
sounds that I've simmered down to predictable range,
a feast of patterning, a treat of tended lines,
and visible forms, toothsome as tenderloins,
to keep you, sucking the images that bring
you close to receive this artful cherishing,
an inexhaustible fountain of passionate waste
while I grow and blossom on its deathy taste.

Postscript:

Watch out, Mrs. Procter, you'll be warmed against your will!
All that jiggling, perverse and thermodynamical,
may suddenly start up again, those turning pages
may tip you right out into life's economic outrages—
and you who have grown so gentle and groomed and tidy
there on the settee, a thoroughly astonished lady
of equilibristic luxury, with a paper plaything,
will burst into metabolic huckstering
and steam back, stoked up on innocent-seeming print,
into devastations, into love's dishevelment.

GRAY'S APOCRYPHA

ON PAGE 1003 of the anatomy text,
in a chapter not used by surgeons and therapists,
consider an illustration, in such pastels
as the heart rarely hears of, shaped like a loose fist,

of the heart. Tubes feed into it from the ear and eye
and fingertips—these are roughly sketched at the margins—
and, tumbling down the tubes, the elements are shown
on their way to the chamber. Some are somewhat like pigeons,

and will flutter and call when they get inside, some
are more like yoyos, running up and down from a fixed
point, but some like oranges roll and peel
and others slip to the bottom like syrup, relaxed.

The heart fills. Each day the heart fills.
In that resonant cave the clutter grows more and more rich,
the calls accumulate, motion reflects from the walls,
there is flight, fall, flurry—finally there is so much

felt that the main valve opens, the heart convulses,
and up a great duct to the mouth it all will pour,
to be mushed there and shaped into words, "dear," "my dear,"
the lips will open and out come "my love," and more.

In the rest of the book our innards came as a shock,
those vacant structures whose juicy dealing hurt
our sense of ourselves—but here it is mostly true.
You know it, I know it, this is what happens in the heart.

And now, on page 1004, consider the heart
in a morbid condition. Those sucking scouts have sent
from out of the air such food as they could find,
and filled the fist. But what awful discontent

the drawing describes! All tubes are clogged, swollen
with stuff, feathers and rotting peels pack
every inch above the sticky bottom,
which is roiled. All movement has batted itself sick

against the growing pressure. What has gone wrong?
See, at the top of the main duct leading out
the trouble's plain. Some outside atmosphere,
unbenign, has sealed the lips. In a great clutch

the heart heaves, and again, to rid itself
of its congestion, then hangs, bulged and sore,
sagging the chest. This will go on. Oh God,
you knew it, I knew it, there is no known cure.

NOTES FROM A SUBURBAN HEART

Freud says that ideas are libidinal cathexes, that is to say, acts of love.
Norman O. Brown

It's TIME to put fertilizer on the grass again.
The last time I bought it, the stuff was smelly and black,
and said "made from Philadelphia sewage" on the sack.
It's true that the grass shot up in a violent green,
but my grass-roots patriotism tells me to stick
to St. Louis sewage, and if the Mississippi isn't thick
enough to put in a bag and spread on a lawn,
I'll sprinkle 5-10-5 from nobody's home,
that is to say . . .

it's been a long winter. The new feeder scared off the birds
for the first month it was up. Those stupid starvelings,
puffed up like popcorn against the cold, thought the thing
was a death-trap. The seeds and suet on its boards
go down their gullets now, and come out song,
but scot-free bugs slit up the garden. It is spring.
I've "made bums out of the birdies," in my next-door neighbor's
    words,
that is to say . . .

your life is as much a mystery to me as ever.
The dog pretends to bite fleas out of sheer boredom,
and not even the daffodils know if it's safe to come
up for air in this crazy, hot-and-cold weather.
Recognitions are shy, the faintest tint of skin
that says we are opening up, is it the same
as it was last year? Who can remember that either?
That is to say,

I love you, in my dim-witted way.

QUEBEC SUITE
for Robert Wykes, Composer

I
EVERY evening
in this old valley
a bird, a little brown bird
says thanks
like a sleepy hen
for red
berries.

II
The farmer sits in the sun
and sends nine kids out to work in all directions.
The baby sits on his lap, the toddler leans on his knee.
We have to buy some fishing worms, *les vers.*
"Vingt-cinq vers, s'il vous plait."
A tow-head boy runs for the can of worms. *"Fait chaud aujourdhui."*
How pleasant it is.
The sun shines on the thin farm.
The lazy farmer beams at his busy children.
We make the dog howl for the baby.
"Ecoute," the farmer tells his child,
"il parle.
Ecoute,
il parle."

III
The dog changes
here in the open, in wild country.
He wanders with chipmunks,
he saw a moose,
birds beset him,
the skunk under the cabin makes his hair go up.
He spreads his toes to walk the dock
over gaps in the boards
and looks at the lake with calculation.
He is another animal.

IV

I am afraid to swim in this water,
it is so thick with life.
One stranger after another
comes out of it. Right by the boat
there rose at dusk the otter,
dark and slick, as if covered with ointment.
I said, "My God, an alligator!"
And the pike comes up, his vacant golden eye
staring away from the hook.
Perhaps there are eels down under,
looking up at the skating bugs.
In Quebec there is no alligator,
but I see many a stranger.

V

The rocky beaches
are covered with blueberries.
I thought they were blue flowers at first.
Now we use them in pie and pancake,
but still they look like flowers.
Hazy blue,
their smoke rubs off with one touch of the finger.
Under that smear
a deeper blue appears,
as rich and dark as anything we earn.
And so this country feeds our hungers.

VI

The loon is yodeling.
My favorite waterfowl, sleek and swarthy,
a master duck,
he will swim under half the lake
before he comes up with his catch, flapping and swallowing.
But strong as he is, brave as he is,
he is a lonesome bird.
He and his mate must touch each other
all day long across the water
with their cries:
"Here. Here I am. And you? You?"
"Yes, I am here. And you? You? You? You? You?"

EARTH TREMORS FELT IN MISSOURI

THE QUAKE last night was nothing personal,
you told me this morning. I think one always wonders,
unless, of course, something is visible: tremors
that take us, private and willy-nilly, are usual.

But the earth said last night that what I feel,
you feel; what secretly moves you, moves me.
One small, sensuous catastrophe
makes inklings letters, spelled in a worldly tremble.

The earth, with others on it, turns in its course
as we turn toward each other, less than ourselves, gross,
mindless, more than we were. Pebbles, we swell
to planets, nearing the universal roll,
in our conceit even comprehending the sun,
whose bright ordeal leaves cool men woebegone.

A GARLAND FOR CHRISTOPHER SMART

I

"For the flower glorifies God and the root parries the adversary.
For the right names of flowers are yet in heaven. God make
gardners better Nomenclators."

FOR COSMOS, which has too much to live up to,
for hyacinth, which stands for all the accidents of love,
for sunflower, whose leanings we can well understand, for foxglove
and buttercup and snapdragon and candytuft and rue,

and for baby'sbreath, whose pre-Freudian white we value,
and for daisy, whose little sun confronts the big one
without despair, we thank good gardeners who pun
with eye and heart, who wind the great corkscrew

of naming into the cork on what we know.
While the root parries the adversary, the rest
nuzzles upward through pressure to openness,
and grows toward its name and toward its brightness and sorrow.

And we pray to be better nomenclators, at home
and in field, for the sake of the eye and heart and the claim
of all who come up without their right names,
of all that comes up without its right name.

II

"For I bless God for the Postmaster General and all conveyancers
of letters under his care especially Allen and Shelvock."

Pastor of these paper multitudes,
the white flocks of our thought that run back and forth,
preserve the coming and going of each nickel's worth
that grazed on the slope of the brain or trotted from its inroads.

And all proxies who step to the door in the stead of the upper
left hand corner, keep coming to every house,
that even the most feeble narration may find its use
when it falls into the final slot of the eye, that the mapper

of human dimension may distend that globe each day
and draw each day the connecting network of lines
that greetings and soapflake coupons and valentines
make between one heart and another. We pray

especially for the postman with a built-up shoe who likes dogs
and the one at the parcel post window who bears with good grace
the stupid questions of ladies, and we especially bless
the back under every pack, and the hands, and the legs.

III

> *"Let Huldah bless with the Silkworm—the ornaments of the Proud
> are from the Bowells of their Betters."*

It was a proud doorway where we saw the spider drop
and swing to drop and swing his silk, the whole
spider rose to raise it, to lower it, fell,
and dangled to make that work out of his drip.

Not speculation, but art. Likewise the honeypot
that makes a fine table, an ornament to bread.
The bees danced out its plot, and feed our pride,
and milked themselves of it, and make us sweet.

And long library shelves make proud homes.
One line, a day in Bedlam, one book, a life
sometimes, sweated onto paper. What king is half
so high as he who owns ten thousand poems?

And the world is lifted up with even more humble words,
snail-scum and limey droppings and fly-blow
and gold loops that dogs have wetted on snow—
all coming and going of beasts and bugs and birds.

IV

> *"Let Jamen rejoice with the bittern blessed be the name of Jesus
> for Denver Sluice, Ruston, and the draining of the fens."*

And let any system of sewage that prospers say,
"I am guide and keeper of the human mess,
signature in offal of who, over the face
of the great globe, moves, and is the great globe's glory."

And any long paving, let it utter aloud,
"I bear the coming together and the going apart
of one whose spirit-and-dirt my spirit-and-dirt
eases in passage, for the earth cherishes his load."

Let drainage ditches praise themselves, let them shout,
"I serve his needs for damp and dryness." Let mansions
cry, "We extend his name with our extensions,"
and let prefabricated houses bruit

their mounting up in a moment to preserve this creature.
Let the great globe, which rolls in the only right air,
say, "He delves me and heaps me, he shapes without fear,
he has me in his care, let him take care."

V

> *"For he purrs in thankfulness when God tells him he's a good cat.*
> *For the divine spirit comes about his body to sustain it in compleat*
>   *cat.*
> *For he camels his back to bear the first notion of business."*

But let those who invest themselves in the dumb beast
go bankrupt gladly at the end of this investment,
for in answering dumb needs he is most eloquent,
but in sickness cannot ask help, and is often lost.

His smell reaches heaven, hope and faith are his fragrance.
Whether he camels his back or barks, he wears our harness,
he sits under our hearts through all his days, questionless.
His tail directs orchestras of joy at our presence.

For his nature he shivers his coat to cast off flies.
For his nature he hisses, or milks the cushion with his claws.
But he will follow our leg forever, he will give up his mouse,
he will lift up his witless face to answer our voice.

And when he burnishes our ankles or turns away from his breed
to sit beside ours, it may be that God reaches out of heaven
and pets him and tells him he's good, for love has been given.
We live a long time, and God knows it is love we need.

A SENTIMENTAL DELUSION

> *. . . There will perhaps be some men we will not love, and some machines to which we will become attached. If we find a being which looks and behaves like other men and is beyond our capacity ever to love, we must say of it that it is only a machine. . . . Should we find a machine which we can love, we must say of it that it has a human nature and human powers . . . I preserve my humanity only so far as I am one who is intrinsically able to love whatever can be loved.*
>
> Paul Weiss, "Love in a Machine Age"

WHEN our hands touched, my darling, suddenly I heard
the ticking of tinny tales, and the only words
left in the room were ours. I looked, and the hard
lights of twelve new machines turned on me and stared.
My friends, my dears, my fellow sufferers
of pulse and gland were gone. These things shed tears
in digits, only the randomizer behind their square
visages made them wander like us, but by wires.

Then, love, for a moment I was lonely. And I knew that pleasures
were up to us. We must taste for those lost others,
consider the rounded world, and kiss among pure
meters preoccupied with heat and pressure.

When, coming closer together, we walked in the streets,
my arm in yours, I heard the noise above my heartbeat
of a hundred roller-skaters, and when I let
my eyes turn from your learning look, only great
steel crates were moving around us. Those strangers in the city
buzzed through their memory banks for some clues to how we
stood, and without a click of analogy
roared by, unprogrammed for such leaning, love's oddity.

And then I understood, dear, that we two were the last
of the sweet speeders, body-snatchers, in a burst
and rush of joy before dark, before all the rest
wheel themselves coldly over our inconstant dust.

My cheek on your cheek, I could never have opened my eyes,
but I heard the whole globe rattle as it rolled in space,
its lands and waters stocked with metallic decoys.
We hold up history single-handed. But it says:
"Life has economies, and can't keep long, as guests
among stiff monsters, two yielding specialists.
Long before you die, chemistry will have you cast
from your little community of two kissing beasts."

So, love, I am afraid of love. Out of the corner of my eye
I watch for us to come uncoupled, for the dread day
when the clinch breaks, we step apart, and are free
to befriend those back to their humanity

who look at us now and see a robot pair
with sensors and effectors clamped together,
claiming our consciousness with clank and whirr,
delivering such data to each other,
that all uncoded comments lose their brightness.
Watt after watt compels us in our kiss,
and men, whose soft veins harden, envy us
our burning circuits, our immortal stress.

PLACET EXPERIRI

"A 96-year-old woman was granted an interlocutory decree of divorce yesterday and said, 'I'll never trust another man as long as I live.'"

The St. Louis Post-Dispatch

To IMAGINE it, to believe it, bring to mind all
that you know of hours and weeks when the speeches fell
on deaf ears, stuffed with suspense or fury, or the wool-
gathering eyes went blind from fluff. Bring to mind what you know
of love that repeats, like songs on the radio,
or of trips when the scenery came either too fast or too slow.

Even thinking of a young gardener who wastes the sense
of his first crocus in waiting to see his first quince,
then rose, then aster, though this only happens once,
will help. A year is gone. Only ninety-five
are left to account for. On the way West, one grave
to the mile, almost, will tell us how much doesn't live

to look back at what it's been through on terrible journeys.
There *are* such journeys. Something of feeling dies,
I swear it dies. And remember that even those
who got to Utah, or beyond, went three miles a day.
What kind of a map could an ant make of a city?
"I'm still alive," is about all they could say,

"the whole point was to get somewhere, and it took some time.
The new life is here, I start now. Nothing is the same."
And as for self-knowledge, everything's slow to strike home.
Give twenty years—twenty-five?—for this sort of thing,
and add that once-in-an-earth-time childhood, a long
unbroken spell of luck in a long morning.

There are plays that don't count, on shipboard and in schools,
and in cracks and corners of the world, unlucky fools
whose daydreams never come true, are never rehearsals.
At forty and fifty the organs of love say my darling,
my darling as sweetly as ever, but they know what is coming.
We must try to explain a hundred years of spring.

There are people who are slow learners and don't know it.
Remember the psychiatrist's story. All his sweat
trying to help a girl, and no go. She sat
one hour a day with hardly a word. Years passed.
He nearly gave up, but the patient said at last,
"I'm getting a lot, but please don't go so fast."

Or consider weeks of bereavement, blank mind,
locked memory. And hours of love when the stunned
ox of a lover circles around a touched hand,
or hypnotizes himself by thinking the name,
the name only, of the other. These too can come
under causes of retardation, being dumb time.

Novels never really happen, and jet flights go
too fearless, too far from the landscape—but no! NO.
Up to seventy, perhaps, but no more. Remember now
a movie scene where the cocky young surgeon repairs
his old mentor, but too carefully, and the heart tires
and stops. He begins to squeeze it, and then one hears

outrageous squeaks of the old muscle, tough
as harness leather. He squeezes and squeezes while the staff
weeps. His wet arm bulges as he works the stiff
thing in his hand with all his strength, but it dies.
What is hard and made, what has clutched and spent every juice,
ends in a rough repetition, but ends painless.

There are plants that, in the hot season, rest
and refill their bulbs. Even without care, they last.
But my God, a *heart,* aflutter in its withered chest—
Think of it, imagine it. Ninety-six years, and the world's
never opened its shell before, oyster without pearls,
insane, obscene, as pink and soft as a girl's.

AN ANNUAL AND PERENNIAL PROBLEM

> *"Among annuals and perennials, there are not many that can proper-ly be classed among these* Heavy *and frankly seductive odors. No gardener should plant these in quantities near the house, or porch, or patio without realizing that many of them, in spite of exquisite fragrance, have a past steeped in sin."*
> Taylor's Garden Guide

ONE should have known, I suppose, that you can't even trust
the lily-of-the-valley, for all it seems so chaste.

The whole lily family, in fact, is "brooding and sultry."
It's a good thing there's a Garden Guide, nothing paltry

about *their* past. Why, some are so "stinking" one expert cried,
" 'May dogs devour its hateful bulbs!' " Enough said.

We'd better not try to imagine . . . But it's hard to endure
the thought of them sitting brazenly in churches, looking pure.

The tuberose fragrance "is enhanced by dusk and becomes"
(remember, they're taken right into some people's homes,

perhaps with teen-age children around in that air!)
"intoxicating with darkness." Well, there you are.

You hear it said sometimes that in a few cases
the past can be lived down. There's no basis

for that belief—these flowers have had plenty of time.
Sinners just try to make decent folks do the same.

What we've always suspected is true. We're not safe anywhere.
Dark patios, of course— But even at our own back door

from half a block off the jasmine may try to pollute us,
and Heaven protect us all from the trailing arbutus!

50

THE GARDENER TO HIS GOD

"Amazing research proves simple prayer makes flowers grow many times faster, stronger, larger."
Advertisement in *The Flower Grower*

I PRAY that the great world's flowering stay as it is,
that larkspur and snapdragon keep to their ordinary size,
and bleedingheart hang in its old way, and Judas tree
stand well below oak, and old oaks color the fall sky.
For the myrtle to keep underfoot, and no rose
to send up a swollen face, I pray simply.

There is no disorder but the heart's. But if love goes leaking
outward, if shrubs take up its monstrous stalking,
all greenery is spurred, the snapping lips are overgrown,
and over oaks red hearts hang like the sun.
Deliver us from its giant gardening, from walking
all over the earth with no rest from its disproportion.

Let all flowers turn to stone before ever they begin to share
love's spaciousness, and faster, stronger, larger
grow from a sweet thought, before any daisy
turns, under love's gibberellic wish, to the day's eye.
Let all blooms take shape from cold laws, down from a cold air
let come their small grace or measurable majesty.

For in every place but love the imagination lies
in its limits. Even poems draw back from images
of that one country, on top of whose lunatic stemming
whoever finds himself there must sway and cling
until the high cold God takes pity, and it all dies
down, down into the great world's flowering.

SESTINA FOR WARM SEASONS

It has been estimated that every seven years or so the body negoti-
ates a complete turnover of all its substance. In other words, your
body does not contain a single one of the molecules that were "you"
seven years ago.

John Pfeiffer, *The Human Brain*

MERCY on us for our many birthdays.
Never again can we envy the lobster for his new room
after the molt, nor any grub his changes.
There is no water in the waterfall
that fell before. Out of the familiar face
a stranger comes to stare every seven years.

But he learns to look like us, we browbeat the years
to repeat, to repeat, and so we waste our birthdays.
Even the astronaut, whose rubber face
slews out of shape as he bursts from the old room,
prays to the wires to hold him and let him fall
back home again, braced against all his changes.

Whoever believes the mirrored world, short-changes
the world. Over and over again our years
let us reconsider, make the old molecules fall
from out of our skins, make us go burning with birthdays.
Inside us, the bombardier may shift in his room
ten times, and may, in the instant his murderous face

peels off to show no murderer there, about-face.
And the earth will say his name each time he changes
his name in mid-air, he keeps its livingroom
open to the coming and going of more years
and of more children who believe in their birthdays.
His missiles mould away and will not fall.

But we were born to love the waterfall
and not the water. By the reflected face
we know each other, never by our birthdays.
Hearts, like lobsters, hide and heal their changes,
for our first self wants itself, and teaches the years
that leak and fill, to reproduce that room.

Even the swollen heart can only make room
for one more self. Dreaming Spring from its Fall,
knee to knee, two sit there and say that years
are all outside, that such absolute face-to-face
stops the spinning story that tells of changes.
And so, my dear, I am afraid of your birthdays.

For love is against birthdays, and locks its room
of mirrors. If your heart changes it will let fall
my face, to roll away in the defacing years.

OPEN LETTER, PERSONAL

*"Dear Mommy. I do not like you any more. You do not like my
friends so I do not like you. I will be away for some months. Love,
Carla."*

Note found in the room of an eight-year-old

MY FRIENDS: If thirty people gather in a room
there is no need for winter heating. For ten years
I have shared your B.T.U.'s, and I think at the same time
of all the summer evenings when fans and airconditioners
were helpless against our being together and our smoke would burn
each other's eyes raw. We are both better and worse
since we met. Better and worse to be warm than lonesome.

Last spring the young writer came again, and we spoke of friends.
But this time he looked at me with his doctor's eyes in his head,
hooded and light like a river turtle's, and talked of their wounds
and drives and systems of aggression, hostility and need,
until I saw them, the skeletons of big fish, stand
around him, bleached and quiet. I am not that safe, I said,
from the hands of my friends, nor are they that safe at my hands.

It is in the strain, in the reaching of the whole mind to see
what it is that is coming toward us, what we are coming toward,
as the earliest essays on Wallace Stevens' poetry
touch and retouch the lines, trying to tell, but the words
are just behind the tip of the tongue—it is there, below
knowledge, before the settled image, that the lovely, hard
poem or person is befriended. Friendship is that sweaty play.

But believe me, my friends, we are in the late essays. A decade
has used us so that when we go out, we are at home.
We know each other's gestures like a book, we can hide
nothing personal but the noises of sex and digestion and boredom,
can leave each other only when we go to bed
or to work—the canvas, the class, the court, the consultingroom,
typewriter or lab. I am trying to say our friendship is dead.

54

Surely the jig is up. We've pinned each other down.
We know which of us will like which new novel, and why,
which of us will flirt, and with whom, and how long it will go on,
which of us are jealous of what in each other, and which fake, or lie,
or don't shave their legs, or don't like cheese, and very soon
your smallest children will tire of naming my couch pillows,
black, white, green, lavender and brown.

And worse: I have seen you betray affection, make a fool
of your mate, and you have seen me. I've watched you cringe and
  shake
and writhe in your selves, and you have seen me in my hospital.
I have given you paper faces and they have grown lifelike,
and you have stuck on my lips in this sheep's smile.
If I could get free of you I would change, and I would choke
this stooge to death and be proud and violent for a while.

As long as the moon hides half her face we are friends of the moon.
As long as sight reaches through space we are fond of the star.
But there is no space, and what light is yours and what is mine
is impossible to tell in this monstrous Palomar
where each pock is plain. I cannot dry you into fishbone
essences, I have grown into your shape and size and mirror.
I think I see you on the streets of every strange town.

We know the quickest way to hurt each other, and we have
used that knowledge. See, it is here, in the joined strands
of our weaknesses, that we are netted together and heave
together strongly like the great catch of mackerel that ends
an Italian movie. I feel your bodies smell and shove
and shine against me in the mess of the pitching boat. My friends,
we do not like each other any more. We love.

A TIME OF BEES

Love is never strong enough to find the words befitting it.

Camus

ALL DAY my husband pounds on the upstairs porch.
Screeches and grunts of wood as the wall is opened
keep the whole house tormented. He is trying to reach
the bees, he is after bees. This is the climax, an end
to two summers of small operations with sprays and ladders.

Last June on the porch floor I found them dead,
a sprinkle of dusty bugs, and next day a still worse
death, until, like falling in love, bee-haunted,
I swept up bigger and bigger loads of some hatch,
I thought, sickened, and sickening me, from what origin?

My life centered on bees, all floors were suspect. The search
was hopeless. Windows were shut. I never find
where anything comes from. But in June my husband's fierce
sallies began, inspections, cracks located
and sealed, insecticides shot; outside, the bees' course

watched, charted; books on bees read.
I tell you I swept up bodies every day on the porch.
Then they'd stop, the problem was solved; then they were there again,
as the feelings make themselves known again, as they beseech
sleepers who live innocently in will and mind.

It is no surprise to those who walk with their tigers
that the bees were back, no surprise to me. But they had
left themselves so lack-luster, their black and gold furs
so deathly faded. Gray bugs that the broom hunted
were like a thousand little stops when some great lurch

of heart takes place, or a great shift of season.
November it came to an end. No bees. And I could watch
the floor, clean and cool, and, from windows, the cold land.
But this spring the thing began again, and his curse
went upstairs again, and his tinkering and reasoning and pride.

It is the man who takes hold. I lived from bees, but his force
went out after bees and found them in the wall where they hid.
And now in July he is tearing out the wall, and each

56

board ripped brings them closer to his hunting hand.
It is quiet, has been quiet for a while. He calls me, and I march

from a dream of bees to see them, winged and unwinged,
such a mess of interrupted life dumped on newspapers—
dirty clots of grubs, sawdust, stuck fliers, all smeared
together with old honey, they writhe, some of them, but who cares?
They go to the garbage, it is over, everything has been said.

But there is more. Wouldn't you think the bees had suffered
enough? This evening we go to a party, the breeze
dies, late, we are sticky in our old friendships and light-headed.
We tell our funny story about the bees.
At two in the morning we come home, and a friend,

a scientist, comes with us, in his car. We're going to save
the idea of the thing, a hundred bees, if we can find
so many unrotted, still warm but harmless, and leave
the rest. We hope that the neighbors are safe in bed,
taking no note of these private catastrophes.

He wants an enzyme in the flight-wing muscle. Not a bad
thing to look into. In the night we rattle and raise
the lid of the garbage can. Flashlights in hand,
we open newspapers, and the men reach in a salve
of happenings. I can't touch it. I hate the self-examined

who've killed the self. The dead are darker, but the others have
moved in the ooze toward the next moment. My God,
one half-worm gets its wings right before our eyes.
Searching fingers sort and lay bare, they need
the idea of bees—and yet, under their touch, the craze

for life gets stronger in the squirming, whitish kind.
The men do it. Making a claim on the future, as love
makes a claim on the future, grasping. And I, underhand,
I feel it start, a terrible, lifelong heave
taking direction. Unpleading, the men prod

till all that grubby softness wants to give, *to give.*